Making Math Easy

Word Problems Made Easy

Rebecca Wingard-Nelson

Enslow Elementary
an imprint of

Enslow Publishers, Inc.

40 Industrial Road	PO Box 38
Box 398	Aldershot
Berkeley Heights, NJ 07922	Hants GU12 6BP
USA	UK

http://www.enslow.com

J
510
W

Enslow Elementary, an imprint of Enslow Publishers, Inc.

Enslow Elementary® is a registered trademark of Enslow Publishers, Inc.

Copyright © 2005 by Enslow Publishers, Inc.

Library of Congress Cataloging-in-Publication Data

Wingard-Nelson, Rebecca.
  Word problems made easy / Rebecca Wingard-Nelson.
      p. cm. — (Making math easy)
  Includes bibliographical references and index.
  ISBN 0-7660-2512-8
  1. Word problems (Mathematics)—Juvenile literature. I. Title.
  QA63.W56 2005
  510'.76–dc22
                                                    2004028097
Printed in the United States of America

10 9 8 7 6 5 4 3 2 1

To Our Readers: We have done our best to make sure all Internet Addresses in this book were active and appropriate when we went to press. However, the author and the publisher have no control over and assume no liability for the material available on those Internet sites or on other Web sites they may link to. Any comments or suggestions can be sent by e-mail to comments@enslow.com or to the address on the back cover.

Illustrations: Tom LaBaff

Cover illustration: Tom LaBaff

Contents

Introduction

Math is all around, and an important part of your life. You use math when you are playing games, cooking food, spending money, telling time, reading music, or doing any other activity that uses numbers. Even finding a television station uses math!

Word Problems Are Everywhere

Word problems use every kind of math. They help you use math to figure out things in the real world. You probably already know how to do the math; now you just need to know how to use it!

Using This Book

This book can be used to learn or to review how to solve word problems. Use it on your own or with a friend, tutor, or parent. Get ready to discover math . . . made easy!

Problem-

Word problems can be solved by following four easy steps.

❶ Read the problem.

Read carefully. What do you know? What do you need to find?

❷ Make a plan.

It is up to you to find the best way to solve the problem. Some problems will give you a plan, like making a table, writing an equation, or drawing a graph.

❸ Solve the problem.

It is time to do the math! If you find that your plan is not working, make a new plan.

❹ Check your answer.

Yay! You are finished, right? Wrong! Always check your answer. Make sure you have answered the right question. Does your answer make sense? Check your math. Mistakes happen to everyone, and a quick double check can help you spot an error.

Solving Steps

Max has three dancing frogs. Li Ming has two. How many frogs do they have in all?

❶ Read the problem.

What do you know?

Max has 3 frogs.
Li Ming has 2 frogs.

What do you need to find?

How many frogs do they have all together?

❷ Make a plan.

You can add to find the total number of frogs.

❸ Solve the problem.

3 frogs + 2 frogs = 5 frogs.
They have 5 frogs.

❹ Check your answer.

Does the answer make sense? *Yes.*
Did you add correctly? *Yes.*

Don't give up!
The first time you try to solve a word problem, it might not work. Keep trying! Look over your work and see if you made a silly mistake, like using the wrong numbers. If you get stuck, try a different plan.

Be positive!
You learn by making mistakes. If you already know all the answers, there is nothing to learn. Remember, it feels great when you finally get the solution!

Use Your Past!
Some of the problems will look like ones you've seen before. Use what you remember from other problems to solve new ones.

Practice!
The more you do anything, the better you become at it. Every problem you solve helps you get ready for other problems.

Solving Tips

Take a Break!

Tough problems can make your head hurt. If you have tried everything you can think of but are only getting frustrated, take a rest. Go to another problem. Go get a snack or a drink. Close your eyes and stretch. Then come back with a fresh brain and try again.

Move On!

Tests can make people nervous. If you get stuck, go on to the next problem. When you answer problems you know first, it helps you get in the test-taking groove. Go back later and do the problems you skipped.

Too Little

When you don't have enough information, you cannot solve a word problem.

Ben bought lunch in the cafeteria for $3.00. Rita only bought a drink. How much more did Ben spend than Rita?

❶ Read.

You know Ben bought lunch for $3.00.
You know Rita bought a drink.
You want to find the difference between what Ben and Rita spent.

❷ Plan.

You can subtract the amount Rita spent from the amount Ben spent to find the difference.

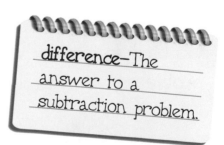

difference–The answer to a subtraction problem.

Information

❸ Solve.

There is too little information to solve this problem. You do not know how much Rita spent.

❹ Check.

Read the problem again. Is the information given, but you missed it the first time? *No.* This problem cannot be solved with the information given.

Too Much

Too much information can make a word problem confusing. Make a list of what you know, then cross out any information you do not need.

Morris has 8 ducks, 2 horses, 3 chickens, a pig, a goose, and 16 cows. How many birds does Morris have?

❶ Read.

You know that Morris has 8 ducks, 2 horses, 3 chickens, 1 pig, 1 goose, and 16 cows.

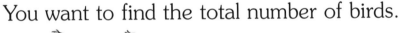

You want to find the total number of birds.

Information

② Plan.

Morris has animals that are not birds, so make a list of all the animals he has. You can cross off any animals that are not birds. Then you can add the numbers of birds to find the total number of birds.

③ Solve.

Morris has   8 ducks,

~~2 horses,~~

3 chickens,

~~1 pig,~~

1 goose, and

~~16 cows.~~

Cross off the animals that are not birds.

8 ducks, 3 chickens, and 1 goose are left.

8 + 3 + 1 = 12 birds. Morris has 12 birds.

④ Check.

Make sure you have not crossed out any birds. Check your addition. Does 8 + 3 + 1 = 12? *Yes.*

Estimation

Some word problems do not ask for an exact answer. An estimate is a good guess that is close to an exact answer.

A guitar pick costs 95 cents. You want to buy 5 picks, and you have 7 dollars. Do you have enough money?

1 Read.

You know that each pick costs 95 cents.
You know you have 7 dollars.
You want to know if you have enough money to buy 5 picks.

② Plan.

The problem asks if you have enough, not the exact amount. You can estimate the cost of 5 picks to decide if you have enough money to buy them.

③ Solve.

Round the cost of one pick to the nearest dollar.

95 cents rounds to 1 dollar.

Multiply by the number of picks you want to buy.

5 picks × 1 dollar = 5 dollars

5 picks cost about 5 dollars. You have 7 dollars. Since 7 is larger than 5, you have enough money to buy 5 picks.

④ Check.

Read the problem again. Did you answer the right question? *Yes.* Check your multiplication. Does 5 × 1 = 5? *Yes.*

Look for

Patterns can help you solve word problems.

Indira put soup cans in rows on a shelf. The top row has 1 can, the second row has 5 cans, the third row has 9 cans. How many cans of soup will be in the fifth row if the pattern continues?

① Read.

You know there is 1 can in the first row.

You know there are 5 cans in the second row.

You know there are 9 cans in the third row.

You want to find the number of cans in the fifth row.

a Pattern

② Plan.

The problem tells you there is a pattern. You can find the pattern and continue it.

③ Solve.

Find the pattern.

Row 1	1 can	Each row has 4 more cans
Row 2	5 cans	than the one above it.
Row 3	9 cans	$1 + 4 = 5$, $5 + 4 = 9$.

Continue the pattern.

Row 4	13 cans	$9 + 4 = 13$.
Row 5	17 cans	$13 + 4 = 17$.

There will be 17 cans of soup in the fifth row.

④ Check.

Does your answer make sense? *Yes.*
Did you add correctly? *Yes.*

Many word problems are easier to solve if you draw a picture to help.

Carol, Jacob, Min, and Ty are standing in line at the movie theater. Carol is in front of Min, Ty is between Carol and Min, and Jacob is behind Min. Who is in the front of the line?

❶ Read.

You know Carol is in front of Min.
You know Ty is between Carol and Min.
You know Jacob is behind Min.

You want to know who is in the front of the line.

❷ Plan.

You can draw a picture of the line to keep all the people in order.

Picture

3 **Solve.**

Draw a line. For each clue you are given, add the clue to the line.

Carol is in front of Min.

Ty is between Carol and Min.

Jacob is behind Min.

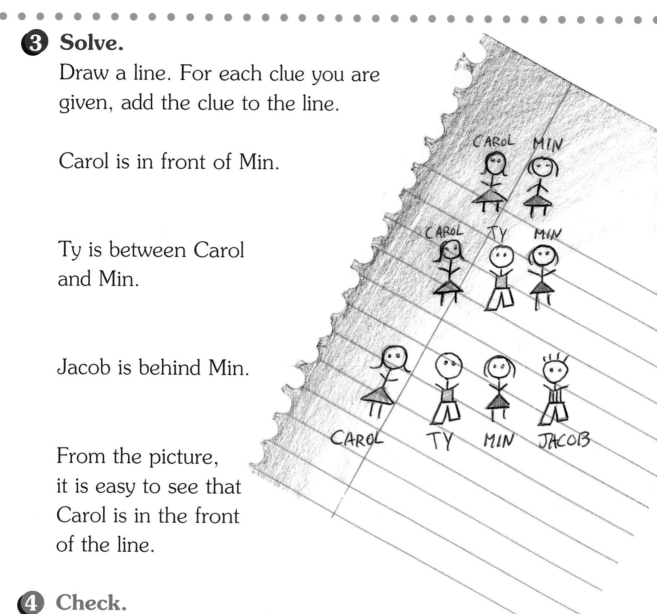

From the picture, it is easy to see that Carol is in the front of the line.

4 **Check.**

Make sure the picture is true for each clue.

Logical

Some word problems can be solved just by thinking about what you know.

Maria has two sons, Tino and Pedro. The ages of all three people are 32, 11, and 8. Pedro is the youngest. How old is Tino?

❶ Read.

You know Maria is the mother.
You know Tino and Pedro are Maria's sons.
You know the ages of the three are 32, 11, and 8.
You know Pedro is the youngest.

You want to find Tino's age.

❷ Plan.

You can use the clues and logical thinking to find Tino's age.

❸ Solve.

Maria is the mother, and parents must be older than their children, so she is the oldest.

Maria is 32.

You know Pedro is the youngest, so he is 8.

Tino is the only person left. The only age left is 11. Tino must be 11.

❹ Check.

Does your thinking make sense? *Yes.* Is there any other age Tino can be, and the clues still be true? *No.*

Organizing information in a table can help you solve some math problems.

Jennifer started with $13 in her piggy bank. For two weeks, she added $3 each week. Then for two more weeks, she added $4 each week. How much money did she have saved at the end of the four weeks?

1 Read.

You know Jennifer had $13 to start.

You know she added $3 each week for 2 weeks.

You know she added $4 each week for 2 more weeks.

You want to know the amount of money she had after 4 weeks.

2 Plan.

You can make a table that begins with the amount Jennifer started with and add the amount she saved each week.

Table

❸ Solve.

Make a table that organizes what you know.

	START	WEEK 1	WEEK 2	WEEK 3	WEEK 4
AMOUNT ADDED		$3	$3	$4	$4
TOTAL SAVED	$13				

Add the amount that was saved each week to the total from the week before.

	START	WEEK 1	WEEK 2	WEEK 3	WEEK 4
AMOUNT ADDED		+ $3 =	+ $3 =	+ $4 =	+ $4 =
TOTAL SAVED	$13	$16	$19	$23	$27

Jennifer had saved a total of $27 after the four weeks.

❹ Check.

Does your answer make sense? *Yes.* Check your addition for each week.

Making a list can help you keep track of information you will use to solve a word problem.

A soccer league uses red or white shorts and blue, red, or white shirts for each team. How many ways can the shorts and shirts be combined?

❶ Read.

You know there are red or white shorts.
You know there are blue, red, or white shirts.

You want to find out how many ways the shorts and shirts can be combined.

❷ Plan.

Make a list of all the different combinations.

❸ Solve.

First list the red shorts with each shirt color.

List

Red shorts   Blue shirt
Red shorts   Red shirt
Red shorts   White shirt

Next list the white shorts with each shirt color.

White shorts   Blue shirt
White shorts   Red shirt
White shorts   White shirt

Now count the total number of combinations.

There are six combinations of shorts and shirts that can be made.

4 **Check.**
Make sure you did not skip any colors on your list.
Count the total number of combinations again.

Some word problems can be solved by starting at the end and working backward.

Bonita spent $3 playing a game at a fair. She won a stuffed rabbit. Her friend gave her $5 for the rabbit. Bonita had $9 after her friend bought the rabbit. How much did she have before she played the game?

❶ Read.

You know Bonita spent $3 on a game.
You know she got $5 for the rabbit.
You know she had $9 after she sold the rabbit.

You want to find how much money she started with.

❷ Plan.

You know what Bonita had at the end. You need to find what she had at the beginning. You can work backward from the end to the beginning.

Backward

③ Solve.

Bonita ended with $9.

Take away the $5 her friend gave her to find how much Bonita had before she sold the rabbit.

$$\$9 - \$5 = \$4$$

Bonita spent $3 on a game. Add the $3 back to find what she had before she played the game.

$$\$4 + \$3 = \$7$$

Bonita had $7 before she played the game.

④ Check.

When you work a problem backward, check the answer by working forward.

Bonita had $7 at the beginning of the fair. She spent $3 on a game.

$$\$7 - \$3 = \$4$$

Then, she sold the rabbit she won for $5.

$$\$4 + \$5 = \$9$$

Bonita had $9 after she sold the rabbit. This matches the problem. The answer is correct.

Make an

If the numbers in a word problem seem too hard, try using easier numbers to understand the problem first.

Four students in Mr. Brooks' class played checkers against each other. Each student won exactly 1 game of checkers. There were no ties. How many games were played?

1 Read.
You know there are 4 students. You know each had won 1 game. You want to know how many games were played.

2 Plan.
Look at a smaller number first and see if you can figure out how to solve the problem.

Easier Problem

③ Solve.

Each time a game is played, there is one win and one loss. Count the number of wins to find the number of games. If there are two students, and each wins one game, then there are two wins, or two games.

$$1 \text{ win} + 1 \text{ win} = 2 \text{ wins, or } 2 \text{ games}$$

Add another student who wins one game.

$$1 + 1 + 1 = 3 \text{ games}$$

For each student who wins one game, one game is played. There are 4 students, so add 1 game for each student.

$$\overset{1}{1} + \overset{2}{1} + \overset{3}{1} + \overset{4}{1} = 4 \text{ games}$$

④ Check.

Does the answer fit the problem? *Yes.*
Is the math correct? *Yes.*

Word problems can sometimes be answered just by knowing how to read a graph or chart.

Which of the nine planets has the most moons?

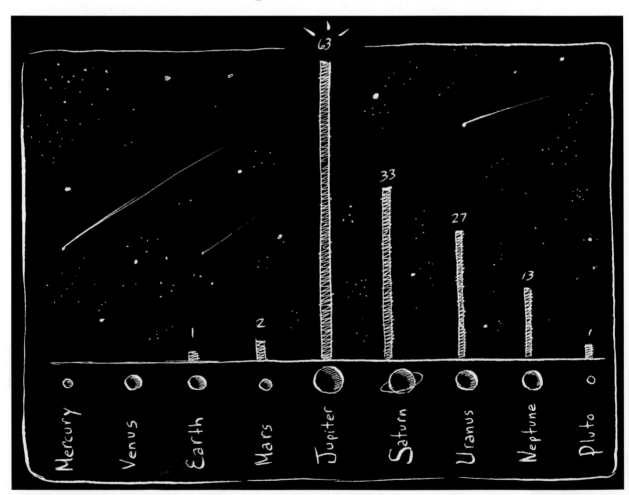

Graph

❶ Read.

You know the number of moons each planet has. You want to find which planet has the most moons.

❷ Plan.

You can use the bar graph to find which planet has the most moons.

❸ Solve.

Look at the bar graph. Which planet has the longest bar? Jupiter has the longest bar, so

Jupiter is the planet with the most moons.

❹ Check.

Read the question. Read the answer. Is the right question answered? *Yes.* Are there any planets on the graph with more moons than Jupiter? *No.*

Some word problems are easy to write as an equation. You can write an equation and then solve it.

equation–A math sentence that uses an equal sign.

Malcolm has 4 computer games. Jim has 7. Malcolm's games plus Jim's games equal Tony's games. How many games does Tony have?

"Malcolm's games plus Jim's games equal Tony's games" can be written using the math symbols + and =.

Malcolm's games + Jim's games = Tony's games

Write in the numbers you know.

Malcolm's games + Jim's games = Tony's games

$$4 + 7 = \text{Tony's games}$$

Do the addition. $4 + 7 = 11$

Check the math. Is $4 + 7 = 11$? *Yes.*

Tony has 11 computer games.

Equation

You may need to write your own sentence before you can write an equation.

Emily wants to buy 3 sets of markers. Each set costs $6. How much money does Emily need?

Write a sentence to describe the problem.

The total cost is the cost of each set times the number of sets.

Write the sentence using math symbols.

The total cost = the cost of each set $\times$ the number of sets.

When in doubt, write it out!

Write in the numbers you know.

The total cost = $6 $\times$ 3.

Do the multiplication. $6 \times 3 = 18$

Check the math. Is $6 \times 3 = 18$? *Yes.*

Emily needs $18.

Addition

Word problems that combine groups use addition.

There are 4 people in the Green family. There are 6 people in the Lopez family. The Green family is staying with the Lopez family. How many people are staying in the Lopez house?

❶ Read.
You know the number of people in the Green family.
You know the number of people in the Lopez family.
You want to find the total number of people in both families.

Problems

② Plan.

You can write an addition equation to combine the two families.

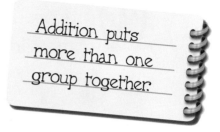

Addition puts more than one group together.

③ Solve.

Write a sentence to describe the problem.

> The Green family plus the Lopez family equals the total number of people.

Write the sentence using math symbols and the numbers you know.

$$4 + 6 = \text{the total number of people}$$

Add. $4 + 6 = 10$

There are 10 people staying in the Lopez house.

④ Check.

Does your answer make sense? *Yes.*
Is the addition correct? You can check addition by using the opposite operation, subtraction.

$$10 - 6 = 4. \text{ The addition is correct.}$$

Subtraction

Word problems that start with a group of something and then take part of the group away are subtraction problems.

There were 12 pieces in a large pizza. Jamal ate 3 pieces. How many pieces are left?

❶ Read.

You know there were 12 pieces in the whole pizza.
You know that Jamal ate 3.
You want to know how many are left.

❷ Plan.

You begin with 12 pieces and take 3 away.
You can write a subtraction equation to find the number of pieces left.

❸ Solve.

Write a sentence to describe the problem.

All of the pizza minus the pieces
Jamal ate is the number of pieces left.

Problems

Write the sentence using math symbols and the numbers you know.

$12 - 3 =$ the number of pieces left

Subtract. $12 - 3 = 9$

There are 9 pieces of pizza left.

4 Check.

Is the right question answered? *Yes.*

Is the subtraction correct? You can check subtraction by using the opposite operation, addition.

$9 + 3 = 12$. The subtraction is correct.

Multiplication

Multiplication combines a number of groups that are the same size.

A box of whistles has 100 whistles in it. A shipping crate has 8 boxes in it. How many whistles are in one crate?

1 Read.

You know there are 100 whistles in a box.
You know there are 8 boxes in a crate.
You want to know how many whistles are in a crate.

Problems

2 Plan.

You are combining boxes with the same number of whistles in each. You can write a multiplication equation to solve the problem.

> When you know the value of one item and you need to find the value of many, use multiplication.

3 Solve.

Write a sentence to describe the problem.

> The number of whistles in a box times the number of boxes in a crate equals the number of whistles in a crate.

Write the sentence using math symbols and the numbers you know.

$100 \times 8 =$ the number of whistles in a crate

Multiply. $100 \times 8 = 800$

> There are 800 whistles in a crate.

4 Check.

Does the answer make sense? *Yes.*
Is the multiplication correct? *Yes.*

Division

Problems that take a group and split it into smaller equal groups use division.

Your heart beats about 4,200 times in an hour. About how many times does your heart beat in a minute?

1 Read.
You know your heart beats about 4,200 times an hour. You know there are 60 minutes in an hour. You want to know about how many times your heart beats in a minute.

2 Plan.
You are taking the total number of heartbeats in an hour and dividing it into beats per minute. You can write a division equation to solve the problem.

Problems

③ Solve.

Write a sentence to describe the problem.

The number of heartbeats per hour divided by the number of minutes in an hour equals the number of heartbeats per minute.

Write the sentence using math symbols and the numbers you know.

$4,200 \div 60 =$ the number of heartbeats per minute

Divide. $4,200 \div 60 = 70$

Your heart beats about 70 times per minute.

④ Check.

Is the right question answered? *Yes.*
Is the division correct? You can check division by using the opposite operation, multiplication.

$70 \times 60 = 4,200$. The division is correct.

Multi-Step

Some problems use more than one operation. Do one operation, or step, at a time.

There are 20 students in fifth grade. Each child chose 2 books in the fall and 2 books in the spring to read. How many books did the fifth-grade students choose in all?

1 Read.

You know there are 20 students in fifth grade.
You know each student chose 2 books in the fall and 2 books in the spring.
You want to find how many total books were chosen by fifth-grade students.

2 Plan.

Books were chosen two times. You can add to find the number of books chosen by each student.

Each student chose the same number of books. You can multiply to find the number of books chosen by the entire fifth grade.

Problems

3 **Solve.**

The students chose 2 books in the fall and 2 books in the spring.

$$2 + 2 = 4 \text{ books}$$

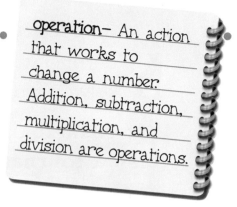

operation— An action that works to change a number. Addition, subtraction, multiplication, and division are operations.

Each student chose 4 books.
There are 20 students.

$$20 \times 4 = 80 \text{ total books}$$

The students chose
80 books in all.

4 **Check.**

Does the answer make
sense? Yes.
Is the addition correct? Yes.
Is the multiplication
correct? Yes.

Combine

You may want to use more than one plan to solve a word problem.

Six basketball teams were scheduled to play a tournament. Each team played each of the other teams exactly one time. Two of the teams did not show up for any games. How many games were played in all?

1 Read.

You know there were six teams all together.

You know two of the teams did not play.

You know each team played each of the other teams exactly one time.

You want to find how many games were played in all.

Plans

2 Plan.

You can first write an equation to find the number of teams that played.

Then you can draw a diagram to help you match up each of the teams that played.

3 Solve.

> 6 teams − 2 teams that did not show up =
> 4 teams that played

Use a dot to show each team. Connect the dots with lines to show each game.

Count the lines.
There are 6 lines.

There were 6 games played in the tournament.

4 Check.

Does a line connect each of the dots to each of the other three dots? *Yes.* Are there 6 lines? *Yes.*

Further Reading

Abramson, Marcie F., Rika Spungin, and Laurie Hamilton. *Painless Math Word Problems.* Hauppauge, N.Y.: Barron's Educational Series, 2001.

Charlesworth, Eric. *225 Fantastic Facts Math Word Problems.* New York: Kane Press, 2000.

Dussing, Jennifer. *The 100-Pound Problem.* New York: Kane Press, 2000.

Helakoski, Leslie, and Sal Murdocca. *The Smushy Bus.* Brookfield, Conn.: Millbrook Press, 2002.

Internet Addresses

Gamequarium. "Problem Solving Games." <http://www.gamequarium.com/problemsolving. html>.

The Math Forum. "Ask Dr. Math." ©1994–2004. <http://mathforum.org/library/drmath/sets/ elem_word_problems.html>.

Index